By the Same Author

The Loosening and other poems
Festivals of Fire
The Turning Path
Farewell and Welcome
Selected Poems 1946
The Palisades of Fear
Adam Unparadised
Collected Poems 1961
Day and Night

Ronald Bottrall

Poems 1955–1973

Anvil Press Poetry
associated with
Routledge & Kegan Paul

Published in 1974
by Anvil Press Poetry
69 King George Street London SE10 8PX
Distributed by Routledge & Kegan Paul Ltd

Clothbound SBN 85646–008–7
Paperbound SBN 85646–011–7

Printed in England
by The Camelot Press Ltd
Southampton

To Margot

'Art thaws even the frozen, darkened soul'

ALEXANDER SOLZHENITSYN
(*One Word of Truth*, The Nobel Speech)

Note

Although this collection of poems covers the period 1955–73, the major part of it was composed between 2nd February and 22nd October 1972. The book was written in Brazil, Greece, Japan, England and Italy.

Some poems have appeared in *The Observer*, *The Times Literary Supplement*, *The Listener*, *New Statesman*, *Encounter*, *The London Magazine*, *Platform*, *Poetry Review*, *The Sculptor and Painter*, *Transatlantic Review*, *New Poems 1960*, *I. W. W. P. Anthology 1972* and in various Brazilian, French, German, Greek, Italian and Japanese magazines. Grateful acknowledgements are made to the editors of these periodicals.

I also have to thank Messrs Routledge & Kegan Paul Ltd for permission to reprint 'William Empson' which appeared in *William Empson: the Man and his Work*; and Arnoldo Mondadori and the author for permission to include translations of two poems by Aldo Palazzeschi.

Contents

5   NIGHTLIGHTS

I   *Early Years*

Talking to the Ceiling

for Eugene Walter

Short-sighted, bent and bald
But full of *bonhomie*,
My father righted himself
Adjusted carefully his pebble spectacles
And leant over the semi-circular counter
To check the weigh-bridge tare
Of tons of gritty coal and coke
Or lengths of timber, oak,
Beech, pine, larch, ash and elm.
The great black stallions meanwhile
Stamping, tossing their manes,
Shaking the ill-made carts
And baring their yellow teeth
Against their foaming bits, jerk
Sharply away from the drivers' whips,
As the figures are double-checked
And meticulously entered
In an ornamental Italian script
Into a long, thick, feint-ruled ledger
Bound in black and lettered gold and red.

I lonely only child played risky games
In the huge timber-yard, shaving past
The spitting circular saws and running
A wood-laden trolley up and down
The gleaming rails or, quite forbidden,
Racing it unloaded at great speed.

Sometimes on public holidays
Or Saturday afternoons
We walked down to the grey-green Atlantic
And watched the sea break into rainbow spray
Against those lofty granite cliffs.
We gaped with fright at the sheer drop

From the incurving top
To the rock bottom of Hell's Mouth.
We picked sea-flowers, pink thrift
With silvery buds, trampled gleefully
Over beds of ling and lichen
And the springing spongy turf,
Climbed down crumbling shale ledges
To look for green, brown-speckled
Gull's eggs, and observed the kittiwakes
Skate through the air, and black-green
Cormorants with sharp hooked beaks
Dive into the waves like thunderbolts.

The headmaster of my father's school,
A local enterprise,
Was the Reverend C. L. Ford B.A., who wrote
Some noted and accomplished hymns.
My father had to leave
Much to his grief and Mr Ford's
At fourteen years of age
When my grandfather,
A former lawyer's clerk,
Fell backwards down the curving stairs
Of his own pub and broke his neck.
At school my father learnt
As well as other things, Latin and French
And just a little Greek.
When I began to learn these languages
I found to my amazement
That he remembered them
In his inimitable way.
Mind you, he knew the Bible
Off by heart, so when I handed him
The New Testament in Greek
And asked him to translate,
He went off in full spate
Once he had found his place.
Greek was no problem

To his fine elephantine memory.

Whenever he had time my father
Went into his cluttered study
Overlooking the rose garden
And fingered books.
Among the chintz-covered chairs
He read the Bible, dipped into
Cruden's concordance
Or took a cursory glance
At an encyclopedia.
He walked to and fro,
Thinking of Longfellow
Ezekiel and Emerson,
From the red plush curtains
To the ink-stained desk
Bulging with unpaid bills,
Hands clasped behind his back,
Meditating and planning
A diatribe against the Pope,
The Scarlet Woman.
Rehearsing too, memorizing
And noiselessly reciting
With moving lips
His polemical, methodical
And evangelical
Sermons, exhorting sinners
To come and kneel with him
At the penitent bench, discard
Their burdens and their trespasses
And be truly and soundly
Converted to the Wesleyan faith.

My father had no spiritual doubts.
He believed in the literal verity
Of every syllable of Holy Writ.
He knew that his own words
Were both inspired and blest.

He was a vessel through whom God spoke.

On wintry Sunday mornings
I often trudged with him
Along muddy byways, across streams
In rain or drizzling mist,
To small grey granite chapels
Where I sat with other worshippers
In the hard pitch-pine pews
To make a congregation.
We knelt in gathering pain
On the cold stone floors
While he, the evangelist,
Wrestled with the Lord in prayer.
His deep bass voice, at first pitched low,
Gradually rose to a sobbing height
Of shuddering hysteria,
Until rivers of sweat
Ran down his temples to his black moustache.

The choir-girls dressed in their Sunday best
Giggled at the holy orator
And stared at me
Archly through half-open fingers
And half-closed eyes. Being shy
I blushed and looked the other way.

The smallest and the farthest of these chapels
Were at Forest and Plantation.
Both lacked trees. But in their stead
Were ruined engine-houses with broken stacks
And rusted iron bobs. The hidden shafts
And adits were cunningly concealed
By overgrowing vegetation.
The landscape looked as if it had been left to rot
Or raped and ravaged by barbarian hordes.

No wonder. After the First World War

When the tin mines failed,
The pillars of the Methodist Church
In Camborne and Redruth
Prompted by fear, full of indecent haste,
Moved all their capital
To the alluvial
Deposits of Malaya
Or Billiton and Bangka.
They left their fellow Cornishman to starve.
In other earlier days
The miners fought the Irish in the streets,
Their battle-cry rang out
'Gib'em Cambern, scat the buggers down',
But now their spirits broke.
Some emigrated as before, some stayed.

In this harsh wind-swept countryside
There always was a friend to give us
A generous heaped-up lunch
Of pasties and pig's fry
And seedy cake,
At some farmhouse nearby
With open drains
And earth closets giving off a stench
That turned my stomach inside out.
But I enjoyed my rompings with the girls
Around the filthy sties and cattle stalls.
Sometimes they lifted up their skirts
And showed their well-curved bums.

Our final hazard was the journey back.
My father often missed the road and so
We got ourselves involved with thorns and thickets,
With bogs and reservoirs and lots of mud.
Whichever way we went we seemed
To wander round into a stream
And end up far from home,
So that high tea was wrecked

Or supper burnt and ruined.

My three anxious mothers watching the clock
Were always furious with him
For dragging a poor delicate child
Through mud for miles and miles
In wretched weather, drenching him to the skin
And depriving him of necessary food.
What particularly annoyed my aunt
Who had a good bump of locality
Was that we mostly travelled
In the wrong direction.
This roused my father's anger
Because, of course, he always knew much better.

He never asked the way.
He merely stated where he was
Or asked a negative question.
'This is Reskajeage Church Town, no doubt?'
When told that it was not
He didn't bat an eyelid.
He painstakingly corrected his informer's
Erroneous style of pronouncing
The name of his own birthplace.
My father would never admit
That he could not improve on
The spelling and pronunciation
Of the ancient Briton.
What did the Celts know
About writing English anyhow?
He thought he had a Norman name
You see, but actually
It came from Brittany.

My father was a man
Greatly respected in the town
For learning and divinity,
And when he saw someone approach

He always raised his hat.
Puzzled, we used to ask,
'And who was that?'
To which he always made the same reply,
'I can't exactly say, but he (or she)
Seemed to know me.'

He had the unusual gift
Of composing his own proverbs.
'An apple in the morning
Is the doctor's warning,
An apple at night
Is the doctor's delight.'
When challenged
Regarding their authenticity
He would reply,
'I heard them when I was a boy.'

My father was an optimist
In most things, especially the weather.
Often when clouds were gathering
And a sou'wester blew
He urged us to take our courage
In both hands and go along
To Porthmeor beach.
We sometimes did, by train.
Eating our egg sandwiches washed down
With dandelion and burdock
We spent the afternoons fully clothed
On the enticing rippled sands
Huddled behind a rock under umbrellas
While the West Cornwall sprinkling rain
A drizzle which he called 'sea mist'
Drenched us to the skin.

His special friend was Cap'n Sammy,
Who lived next door
And ran the men who tended buddles,

And women too, 'Bal maidens, if you please.'
Also the Boys' Brigade
All covered in marmalade.
Leading the files as commandant,
In khaki shorts and Anzac hat,
His little bow-legs twinkled.
But after forty years of friendship
There was no change.
They raised their hats, one to the other,
'How are you, Mr Bottrall, how d'ye do?'
'How are you, Cap'n Sammy, what's the news?'

If ever I was guilty of a peccadillo,
Which in those days I thought to be
A mortal sin against the Ten Commandments,
In order to escape a beating from my father,
That hurt him more than it did me,
Or so he said (I was less sure of this)
In the wash-house or in the cellar,
I used to try two subterfuges.
One was to step furtively on Togo
A very noisy Pomeranian,
Just when the argument was getting heated.
His barks and screams increased
The general babel and, with a bit of luck,
In the confusion he got the blame.
Should this ruse fail, I usually could find
One of my four parents
To side with me against the rest.
The verdict then was bound to be
'Not proven'.

A travelling evangelist Penfold by name
Set up his tent in Camborne Town
When I was nearly ten.
Night after night among the choirboys
I sang the hymns
And every time 'I'm praying for you'

Resounded through the tent I felt a qualm.
A boy beside me in a fine soprano sang
The words each night for me, he said.
Eventually I went
To the penitential bench
Confessed my sins
And praised the Lord
Although I had suspicions
From the age of six that all I heard
About Him and His Father didn't exactly fit.
The Holy Ghost I couldn't grasp at all.

When I was eleven years old
I was enrolled
In the Cadet Corps of my school.
Standing at ease one afternoon
I felt the master's swagger-cane
Striking with considerable force
My aching putteed legs.
I yelped with pain.
Day-dreaming in my usual way,
Quite innocently, unafraid,
I was eating a banana on parade.

Our favourite family walk was down
To the North Cliffs, our nearest sea,
An awesome spectacle of jagged capes
Jutting three hundred feet or more
Into the salty heathered air. The road
Went to the White Gate, then a path
Between the pinewood-sheltered manor house
And the eighteen-acre field
Led through the tin-streams
With their bright red rivers
To a clear gravelly trout stream
Which ran towards Bell Lake.
One day when I had Togo on the lead
Beside the stream, he jumped right in

And I, I can't think why,
Clung to the lead and staggered
After him till I was floundering
In water eighteen inches deep
And well above my trousered knees
Much to the delight of my accompanying friends.
Thereafter I was always known as Hero.

At St Ives in the summer days
I helped a fisherman called William,
A distant relative on my grandma's side,
To take the tourists round the bay.
My greatest joy was to be allowed
To hold the tiller and help sail the boat
And catch the quick inquisitive mackerel
With their blue-green scales
Gleaming and rippling in the sun.
More often it was rowing
And tough work that could be
When the wind blew dead against the tide,
For William was getting on
And after a hard winter's fishing
Was none too active.
Sometimes I got sixpence
Sometimes a shilling
Sometimes a few words of praise.
Then the long row back began
To Porthminster's golden sand.

A charming little girl
Called Vyvyan Hilary Harvey
Who lived across the road
Died of tuberculosis at the age of seven.
Six youths were chosen
To be her bearers. I was one.
All were nearly six feet tall
And nearly all were cousins.
We travelled in a wagonette

To the church in a small village,
Praze, where my Dad was born,
Some seven miles away.
I was the last to leave the wagonette
And as I moved back
Towards the rail and step
The frisky horse shot forward
And so did I.
Falling I grasped the rail, performed
An unpremeditated somersault
And landed on my feet
Trembling in every nerve and limb.
What filled me with fright
Filled them with laughter
Barely suppressed and up the aisle
The tiny coffin rocked its way.

At the end of our long fruitful garden
The allotment abutted on our wall.
Jumping over we manned a sanded trench
Or sat as sentinels in a small hut at its end
Playing at being soldiers.
There when my puberty began to trouble
I took solitary refuge
And consulted an old medical book
To find out what was happening, and what
These liquefying nightly dreams might mean.
Urged on no doubt by my poor worried mother
My father called me one day to his study
In a sepulchral voice.
'You have been reading in this book?'
I stuttered, 'Yes.' 'And looking at
These photographs and drawings?' 'Er, yes,'
My dried-up palate and my quivering vocal chords
Tremblingly announced. Silence.
A long-breathed silence filled the room.
'Then,' said my father, 'you must know
All that there is to know about these things,

But remember, to the pure all things are pure.'
The interview was at an end
And I was left as ignorant as before.

My father used to stay up late at night
Ostensibly to read theology.
Instead he roamed about the house,
Sampling a few novels or detective fiction,
Reading for some strange reason
The last chapter first.
His night cap was a nip
Of any medicine that lay around.
'What's good for them', he thought, 'will do me good.'
One night my Aunt and Ann
The wife of Cap'n Sammy and herself a nurse,
Put in a bottle among other things
A triple dosage of cascara.
Here we must draw a veil
Over three days in bed or, rather, out.
They cured him all right.

As a result of this night roaming
He sometimes nearly missed
His breakfast of sultana cake and tea.
When we searched we usually found
Him kneeling on the floor,
His bare legs sticking out
From his old flannel nightgown,
His head bent on the bed.
He had dropped off to sleep
While saying silently his prayers.

Religious rites are very fine and proper
Within the limits normally prescribed.
But there are limits.
When we received a black-edged letter
That took six weeks to come by water
Announcing that a nephew we had never seen

Had died, we were instantly immured
Behind Venetian blinds
In total darkness, not allowed
To move or speak, except in dire necessity,
For four and twenty hours.
It made my mother weep.

My father never thought of dancing
As an art, or even a social grace;
To him it was an impure act
If not downright licentious.
He raged and raised his rhetoric against
The Turkey Trot and the Bunny Hug
As verging on the obscene.
When my aunt asked if he had ever seen
Or could describe these bestial capers
He would reply, 'I've never witnessed them
And please God never shall,
But I've read about them in the newspapers
And that's enough.' Then he'd go off
To the Saturday Night Prayer Meeting
Which he often led,
Or to the barber's shop,
To cleanse his mind from thoughts of sin and shame.

Music was just another trial.
My father sang in monotone
And could not tell whether the tune
Was 'God Save the King' or 'Pop goes the Weasel'.
People stood for the first
Which helped him quite a lot.
I loved the gramophone with its great horn,
His Master's Voice, but the wrong Master,
As I soon found, and the wrong sound,
Quite unlike hymns.
One Sunday absentmindedly
I put on my favourite piece,
The Bally Coppélia,

And was severely punished.
Fairly enough, I thought.
I'd used a dirty word
Upon the Sabbath Day.

Most difficult of all were meals at home,
Cooked on a Cornish range
Which warmed the kitchen.
My father and my grandmama
Always addressed each other
In the third person. If things were going well,
'Frank' and 'The Grannie',
But sometimes when the atmosphere was tense
Just 'he' and 'she',
While looking at the ceiling.
They had been doing this for years.

My grandmother, my mother's mother,
Wore a rich tunic of black bombazine.
Born in a hovel with four rooms
And with no running water,
She took great pride in having lived
In mansions she had never seen.
Nothing was good enough for her.
But she was tough and spry
With not a grey hair on her jet-black head
At seventy odd.
She had nailed cardboard soles
On to her sons' dilapidated boots
To get them off to school,
And cut their leather laces
From remnants of a farrier's apron.

Although she never learned to write
Or even shape the letters of her name,
My Grannie read the Bible every night.
She had a formidable memory
Of things that happened in her infancy;

Often she recalled how, as a girl,
When she was nearly ten years old,
A sailor from the Falmouth packet boat
Brought the heartening news to Hayle
That the Crimean war was won.
Throughout the town a garbled message spread,
'The Old Sevastapool is dead!'

She ruled her daughters
With an iron hand.
At the first sign of insubordination
She would go up to her room
In indignation,
Dress up in her black finery
Jet beads and all
And tie on her best bonnet.
When asked where she was going
She would reply,
'Down to the Workhouse
To end my days in peace.'

One sultry noon at Sunday lunch
Passions ran high,
About some minor point of Hebrew history.
And then The Grannie's voice
Came crystal clear,
'Why do we never have family prayers
Here in this house?
Frank, the great preacher,
Works to save every soul, except our own.'
A terrifying hush ensued.
My father frowned, the ceiling creaked,
All nature was subdued.
My mother and my aunt
Sat still and listened dumbly.
They were not quite holy enough
To join in these oblique
Religious conversations,

And I was much too young.

A dialogue between a Holy Man
And an equally Holy Woman,
Both talking to the ceiling
Is hardly healing.
It is more like a couple of star-gazers
Cutting each other's throat with razors.

Notes

This poem covers, roughly speaking, the years 1914–20.

Page 19, lines 11–13: *The Irish riots took place in Camborne, Cornwall, in 1873 because of the introduction of Irish labourers into the mines by a Roman Catholic family called Pike*. Scat, *a word of many meanings, here means* knock.

Page 21, line 33: *The Cornish* bal capuns (*mine captains*) *were highly regarded and had quite an important position in society. Mr Samuel Williams owned a tin-stream works, which was a much lower kind of business. The application to him of the title* Capun *or* Cap'n *was therefore slightly ironical.*

Page 22, line 1: Bal *means mine. The women usually did the heavy work of* spalling, *breaking up the tin or copper ore, but they also in the* streamers (tin streams) *looked after the* buddles *or* ruddles, *a frame of iron bars bearing some resemblance to a gridiron, which separated out the tin ore from the stream.*

Page 22, lines 20–21: *Our Pomeranian was called after Count Heihachiro Togo (1847–1934), Admiral in command of the Japanese fleet during the war of 1904–5, when Japan defeated Russia.*

Page 29, lines 1–7: *My grandmother was born near Hayle, Cornwall, on 2nd October 1845, so that she was within a few weeks of her tenth birthday when the French, on 8th September 1855, established themselves in the Malakoff at Sevastopol, thereby virtually ending the Crimean War. The upper road at St Ives, where I spent all my childhood summers, has a belvedere overlooking the harbour, called The Malakoff.*

2   *Time and Place*

First Anniversary

for Margot

Your valiant beauty, stronger than a vice
Shoots holy particles through my dull halm
And leaves my heart without a cicatrice.

Bombarded day and night by this dread balm
My proud flesh liquefies and knits again
The prouder for its chafed baptismal calm.

Bodies can speak more loudly than the rain
Plumb deeper than a subterranean fire
And teach more quickly than a frosty pain.

By fire we are preserved from the foul gyre
That kindles, fridges and consumes its being
In selfish heat and cannibal desire.

Our fire is leech that fills our veins with saying
Giving our eyes the tenderest of touch
And sensitizing hands to delicate seeing.

The flame creates a little more than much
Seals the fallacious surgery of the knife
And mollifies the cross into a crutch.

We owe each other love, I owe you life
Transfused with blood that carries in its plasm
The how of joy, the whatness of all-wife.

Our lightning splits time with an instant chasm
Making the pulsing world stand heartbeat still
And spans eternity in a spasm.

Lovers can charm the poisonous wastes that kill
Those who too dry to weep shed envious tears.

Daily with clasping hands we mount a greener hill.

Whispers unheard save us from earthly fears,
Our single night breeds glories in a glance
And starlight is the measure of our years.

We weave the figures of our burning dance
Across the poles and tease the moon to sing
Those lunar melodies that bring a trance
When desire is a hawthorn song on a May morning.

Copacabana 1955

Down the magnificent beach of silver sand
Divided regularly, band after band,
By runnels of brown water from the sewage pipes,
Walk three women and three men, society types,
In evening dress, mink and top hats. Carefully they light
A ring of candles. The women dressed in white,
The men in tails, enter the treacherous sea,
Encounter the slow-falling combers gingerly,
Breakers that crash like thunder and jet their cloud of spray
Upwards for sixty feet. The Cariocas stand and pray.

It is now midnight. Under a shimmering full moon
Which has seen scores of foolish swimmers drown
They have left their chauffeur and their Cadillac
By the wave-patterned marble pavement, no lack
Of money there. They strew, up to their waists in tepid sea,
Black and gold banded wreaths of flowers reverentially,
And then return to light more candles in the beach's heart.
Stately as ever, they and the Cadillac depart.

Amazonian Scene

In the hot writing jungle outside Manáus
Where almost everything is green
Or melts into green shades
I was talking, stifled by flies, about poetry
To a debarred Brazilian magistrate
In his disordered bedroom,
An Old Etonian has-been
Slung high up in a hammock,
Once a Protector of Indians
Now an indefatigable writer
Of hundreds of elegant sonnets
In English and Portuguese, fiercely guarded
And locked up securely in iron boxes.

As I approached his ramshackle house
There suddenly appeared
A graceful girl with olive-green skin
And arrows in her light green hair.
She glided off, unseen perhaps
By him I thought, while I stood and stared,
Perturbed by this phenomenon.

'Who or what was it that I saw?'
'My wife, an Indian princess.'
We talked about Petrarch, Michelangelo,
Wordsworth, Hérédia and Camões.
He had a good poetic ear and a keen eye
But as far as I could tell
He hadn't noticed that his wife was green.

Hellenics

for Roma Gill

When George Gordon Noel Lord Byron was trailing
The pageant of his bleeding heart through the brothels
And palaces of Europe Greece was ailing.
Visionary men called him to leave his hot hells,
Teresa and La Fornarina, and lead the few
Who had little or no idea of what to do.
Crossing from Cephalonia in a mystic boat
He cut his gaudy words to fit a Souliot coat
And led the wrangling Greeks and Philhellenes
Across the myth into more muddled scenes.
As mediator but not quite, Byron's brigade
Quashed the fool traitors who had squared the Turks.
He caught a cold while shivering to their aid
And perished in his faith, showing no soldier's works.
Byron, the great *Veeron*, flared on and on
To national mourning at the Parthenon
Salutes of guns, the Abbey, stone on stone,
And the first instalment of the London loan.

*　　　*　　　*

They fought. And again. The Philhellenes
The common soldier fought in Crete
In the sparkling Cyclades, at the Hellespont
In the marshes of Missolonghi.
For what? A handful of foxes, a breath
Of dust, and a private right to die.
Unquiet graves shifted by bureaucrats
From rock to rock, island to island,
Among the scattered drums of history
Among wrecked columns and ruined altars
Among the cypresses edging the metal sun.
'In the middle of war, think of it! Poetry!'
The poetry of deceived girls, incest

Floating rudderless in seas of poison,
Passion, flights of swans,
Innocent butterflies in the breeze,
And freedom, always the traitor word 'freedom'.
That is how the Hellenes saw poetry.

      ★   ★   ★

The poetry of life and death the Greeks lived
On two sharp levels like the Byzantines.
Poetry and truth at different levels.
Truth observed by their shrewd ancient eyes
And ideal truth created for the eyes of others.
These warring truths cut the Greek mind in half
And left the Hellenes looking strangely like
Double-crossers to mis-hellenic foreign eyes.
The Mis-hellenes failed to grasp the meaning
Of ideal truth, the ethnic truth of Greece. The truth
That finds brigands 'noble klefts' and
The Dilessi murderers not Greeks but vile Wallachians.
To the instructed eye there are other truths
Deep poetic truths in the descendants of the Byzantines.

      ★   ★   ★

The old man with the elegant parentheses
In educated Alexandrian Greek, or English,
Or French, that always turned, eventually,
Into an ordered piece of observation,
Was enjoying his venal and exciting loves
For the bodies of boys. Out of these bodies
Were born satraps, barbarians and emperors,
Young kings embroidered with amethysts and pearls,
Dynasties of poetry fuming from the garbage
And gutters of Alexandria. Alexandria whose music
Never departed. Alexandria to whom he could not say farewell.

The old man forgot the big-bellied bees on the thyme,

The asphodel, the purple fade-out of Hymettus,
Forgot the hived Mycenean tombs, the small voice
Of the water-turtle on beaches in the Sporades
And the bronze nakedness of Athenian day.
Cavafy did not forget. He had no need to remember.
He had no need of these luxuries.

Ignoring the small warring states and
The Greece that exists as a schoolroom plug
Or a smudged tear in a don's eye
He created a city of the living tongue
The tongue of the Greece that we know,
The Greece of broken pavements and broken promises.
He gave blood to ghosts and became an era.

★   ★   ★

Give me your hands, warriors and poets,
Rest them in the new marble quarries.
Broken regiments marching along blind roads
You have died for a myth of history.

Love in Umbria

For years on my teenage bed between farm, sea and mine
    I saw through the Medici books a new life
Of grape-vines, cupolas, fig-leaves, olives and porticos,
    Ancient hill towns with garlanded white oxen
Pious and gentle, the Fonti del Clitunno
    Whose classical crystal waters bordered by
An intense green gush in a sudden flowering,
    Sloe-eyed maidens surrounded by fauns and satyrs
Bathing and splashing naked in the scented pools of love.

At twenty-one I went to that dark hilly city
    Perugia, Etruscan, Gothic, but not gay,
And on a vast sweating flea-ridden bed encountered
    My first love, blonde, blue-eyed, full-breasted, long-legged
Mary Manin, from Istrian Pola, famed for its Roman
    Amphitheatre and Golden Gate, who taught me
In her analytical affectionate Slav way
    That Italy was much more mountainous than meadow,
So Italy became my spiritual father, not my mother.

Attic Shepherd

Among the porcelain of my childhood dream
A tip-toe figure crook in hand curves on
Quickly as silver through the window-frame
Of odes and fables, elegantly gone

To satisfy a shepherdess's whim
Through all the hoops and farthingales of passion.
How I envied him, able to print those prim
And proper lips in true bucolic fashion.

Now the sweet sour smell of sweated leather
And clothes hanging heavy as a wet fleece
On the patched cob walls in the scrawny heather

Shape me a shepherd ragged at the knees
Bones crying out from the frost-bitten weather
With a dried-up past, no present, and no peace.

Giorgio Morandi Speaks

for Patrick Hayman

That's my last bottle hanging on the wall.
Observe the delicate stretched neck, a fall
Of shoulder so intimately feminine
And rounded contours priming a line
Of isolation bounded by a final calm;
Long necks like pinetrees in Emilian light
Docile and dry, the ochred ground a psalm
Patiently harmonizing space and height.
By brushing objects away from your eyes
I have filled a gap in your memories.

Venice Submerged

You who once held the gorgeous East in fee
Can only keep your head above the water
For half a century. The indifferent sea
Tugs at your foundations, steamers batter
Your ancient walls. To be or not to be
Is hardly a question. The tycoons who matter
Don't care a damn for your mortality
As long as their fat bank accounts get fatter.

In fifty years a few revenants old and gray
Will watch tankers pollute your grave until their hulls
Dip on the horizon. Splendour has fallen away.
Drowned cupolas of St Mark are crowned with skulls.
Garlanded with seaweed the bronze horses neigh
Below the slime of pigeons and the scream of gulls.

Ups and Downs of Politicians

I was going to the City to consult my broker
When I took a quick drink at my pub, the Blue Boar.
Along came a Rolls-Royce. The man next the driver
Was pale as a person pursued by the Furies.
His friends and relations inside the car
Seemed to be taking leave of him and his life.
I wondered who he was, he looked very important.
The people in the pub told me that he had been
Chancellor of the Exchequer for several years
When things were going well for himself and his friends.
His salary was around ten thousand a year
And at least three times a month the Prime Minister
Visited him at his country estate. Yesterday
His was one of the most esteemed names in the land;
A lovely wife and beautiful children. Today
The Prime Minister summoned him to 10 Downing Street
And asked him to apply for the Chiltern Hundreds.
He had compromised himself with a Soviet dancer
And denied this when questioned in the House.
So it is with those who hold the highest offices:
Fame and wealth one minute, obscurity the next.
After his retirement to a much smaller house
He sometimes thought of his great days, but he took up
Social work to ease his conscience. His chief preoccupation
Was to keep his mind at peace among the low hills
Where his orchard bore good fruit, the shrubs were trimmed
And the lawn was well-mown, green and level.
Can anyone doubt that this was the best ending?

Roundabout

The woman turned and looked back.
    She became a pillar of salt.
The man turned and looked back.
    He lost his wife.
The boy turned and looked back.
    He lost his future.
The girl turned and looked back.
    She lost her honour.
The climber turned and looked back.
    He lost his foothold.
The M.P. turned and looked back.
    He lost his seat.
The priest turned and looked back.
    He lost his faith.
The King turned and looked back.
    He lost his head.
The Prime Minister turned and looked back.
    He sold his memoirs for millions.

St Austell

Against the tortured zigzag patterns
Of ancient splintery rock spring
Great white pyramids, the shining
Mounds of gravel waste from
China-clay pits dehumanizing man
To the cacophonic cries of terns
That sound across Veryan bay
As far as the fashionable golf course
Packed with the detritus of humanity.
Deep, forsaken pits of blue-green water
Testify to a long-dug day
Of horny hopeless working hands
And indelibly endorse
Their blank cheques of mortality.

Ballade

for F. T. Prince

The sea at evening moved across the strand
When you watched soldiers in a bestial war
Bathe naked to feel free on alien sand
From bonds of death and animality.
Your soldiers in the sea asked you for more
Than you could give of immortality
To men destined to cut and hack and die.
War is rage, hatred, bitterness and gore.

A soldier is a kind of tool at hand
For those who talking go from door to door
To keep the fires of patriotism fanned.
The soldier lured to take his lethal fee
Finds patriotism is a specious whore.
Hold a long spoon when you invite to tea
The devil in all his martial panoply.
War is rage, hatred, bitterness and gore.

Whatever price your future may demand
Remember the pain the Tuscan artists bore
When they showed Christ falling at his last stand
For the redress of our humanity
And painted him on the cross with scar and score.
Reading his pallid flesh you then could see
The depth of our sad world's iniquity.
War is rage, hatred, bitterness and gore.

Envoy

Prince, it is time to try your artistry
On some new noble theme you have in store,
Greater than war or your biography:
Peace that floods in from God's eternal shore.
War is rage, hatred, bitterness and gore.

Two Poems of Aldo Palazzeschi

(*born 2 February 1885*)

1. Pornography

Taken by this thing
So much talked about
The wish comes to everyone
To see what it is,
And getting for myself certain magazines
Which publicize this tedious argument
I could even admire on the cover
A woman as Our Lord made her
And he didn't do badly
To tell the truth.
And inside others competed
To exhibit completely
Their exuberant beauty.
And a man and a woman as well,
Who seemed ready for that act
Commanded by Our Lord
In order that our species should not be extinguished.
So much that at this point
A suspicion flashed through my mind
Whether the real pornographer
Was not the Creator of humanity.
Having arrived at a more accessible peak
I said to myself:
'In the end I have understood: pornography is only the truth.'

2. Futurism

Sixty years away
From the Milanese-Florentine movement
I often hear people talking eagerly about Futurism.
They speak with genuine curiosity
Serenely and with a benevolent smile
Frequently with enthusiasm
Particularly the young
Who rush at what survives
To examine documents
Receive information and fresh news
About this wholly unknown
But immensely topical phenomenon.
After the furious ostracism which greeted
Futurism from its birth
The whole thing seems amazing
Like nothing on earth;
Instead it is perfectly natural
And in no way surprising.
Futurism could only be born in Italy
A country which always looks backwards
In an absolute and exclusive way,
Where only the past is contemporary.
This is why today Futurism is all the rage
Because Futurism too is part of the past.

from *Via delle cento stelle*
    (September 1972)

Olympics

for Charles Tomlinson

Asleep among heedless weeds I
Awake beside a bayonet.
Grass, cold crowner of the dead,
Bless the roots of memory.

Bells tear the steeple from the church
And die in overtones of metal.
Brass relates the reverent mail
Of knights who felled a sepulchre.

Death has his rivalries, like life,
But death-in-life is merely
Envious of death and life.
Gods vie immortally.

The sculptor, hewn from rock
Scales the abyss of doubt and
Hackles raised, crows like a cock
Preening his bloody spurs.

On lawns of ice the architect
Of passion builds pavilions
Glittering with lion eyes
And the spectrum of spring suns.

Tomorrow will kindle a torch
In the athlete's harvest hand
And the poised javelin
Will strike root in friendly land.

Sestina: Dream is Reality

for Peter Jay

When young our lives are centred on a dream
Which has no contact with reality;
Our need above all other things is order
On this disordered planet we call earth.
Lacking this rule our world will end in sorrow
And we shall be ejected from the garden.

Weeping will never keep us in the garden,
We must take arms against our lulling dream
And free ourselves from the burden of our sorrow.
By grappling fiercely with reality
And bringing despised commonsense to earth
We can achieve a beneficial order.

Where are the men who will obey an order
To till and fertilize our barren garden
With seedling soil and fructifying earth
Instead of lying fallow in a dream?
Face to face we should not fear reality
Or let ourselves be overcome by sorrow.

There are many ways to transcend sorrow.
If worst comes to the worst we give an order
For tots of rum to drown reality
And forget our dead friends buried in war's garden.
We tune ourselves to find fresh wavelengths, dream
Of a new paradise we will create on earth.

Knowing but little of happenings on our earth
Why should we sink ourselves in floods of sorrow?
Would it not suit us just as well to dream
And let disorder strike down rigid order?
Why should we bother to design a garden
When we cannot define reality?

If we endure too much reality
Our human frailty dissolves in earth.
It may prove best to cultivate our garden
Leaving the others to shoulder the world's sorrow
And think back through our ravelled lives in order
To catch the beauty of our childhood dream.

Our dream may turn out your reality.
What you call order may not come on earth.
The men of sorrow may preserve our garden.

Blind Obelisk

I stand on the purple-heathered Cornish hill
Carn Brea which heaves its dragonish
Druid length slowly along
From Redruth my school-time-town
To Camborne where I began to breathe,
Looking at layers of civilization
The work of unknown neolithic men
Recently dug up and catalogued,
Beside the Basset family monument
To eighteenth-century Lord de Dunstanville
Who probably knew nothing of these exciting things
Or cared, though much had been uncovered in his time.
The thousand-pound great granite obelisk
At least recalls the ten-pound annual grant
To miners blinded in the Basset mines.

Peak Picasso

The bull has hit the bull's-eye
And Joan Miró's toreador rises
As his black widow gropes away
Into the air above beautifully
Arranged blobs of colour
Like a grasshopper or an astronaut.
Picasso a wittier and weightier
Matador has hit the jackpot on earth.
Millionaire Manolete bit the dust;
Multi-millionaire Pablo Picasso
Eats bulls for breakfast.

Under cover of overlapping and contrasting
Honeycombed planes Picasso promenades
Over his friend and gradually achieves
The disintegration of D-H. Kahnweiler
Disrupted in three dimensions.
In this rippling dismemberment
Picasso finds his own present
And his own reality.
The scattered parts of Kahnweiler's body
Combine to create a populous city.

Andalusian Picasso understands
That destruction is the magical source
Of creation and of life
The healing wound that never closes.

★   ★   ★

Now that he is dead he is with us.
An Everest culminating in despair
Has vanished from the horizon
Undefeated and unscaled.

Creepy-crawly

'We walk backwards into the future
Looking forwards into the past.'
Do we Mac? Of course not
You mesmeric old word-plugger.
We crawl blindfold whichever way
We may happen to be going or looking
From the beginning to the end.

Over the Years

In years of blighted murphies and murrain
     Top dogs barked their wares.
Plausible Germans pushed Henkel champagne
     And dark Munich beers.
Mad Irish scraped the bottom of the pot
     In rags and hiked it
While the imperialist British got
     The loot and liked it
The cultured French regarded with disdain
     The unlettered rest
Hermetically sealed in their own brain
     So obviously best.
Gastronomic Dutchmen drank their dinner
     In a classic booze
While Italians tried to spot the winner
     So as not to lose.
Belgians in Cadillacs hit the cobbles
     With no speed limit
And with terrifying dronken wobbles
     To show their spirit.
The cagey Danes did all they could to save
     Their precious bacon.
Sometime between the cradle and the grave
     Luxembourg might waken.

Now friend and enemy, have-not and have,
     Freed from history
Unite in one great loving family.

The Nine

for Brian Morris

The nine blind men
Each with his hands around
The next one's throat
Stand in a ring
Waiting for the squeeze
That may not come.
A spiritual deadlock.
Broken each will feel
The strangling hands
Of the next man
And see hell or paradise.

Hardy Revisited

'Any little old song
Will do for me.'
The poet was wrong.
Faces he loved to see
And joys not to be,
But no new song
No modern theme
On which to play.
So he was left alone
That winter day
With ash leaves gray
And a world of bone;
Without a gleam
To undeceive his dream,
Just the sun's gloom
In a dark room.
He stood on Beeny Head
With hope dead
And feeling fled,
One phantom figure
Left to allure;
No vibrant strings
Only sad heart-stirrings.
A man to praise
For his yesterdays.
A man of farewells,
Partings and knells,
A man of sorrows
Acquainted with grief
And the withered leaf,
With no tomorrows.
A full look at the Worst
Chidden of God,
Is the letter curst

Not the spirit raised;
Good under the sod
Is no way to Better,
However praised.

Weep not for Dylan Dead

Rave not against the dying of the light.
Casting our shadows into Plato's cave
We must accept the trauma of the night.

The blind bitter end always is in sight
However much of hopefulness we have.
Rave not against the dying of the light.

Bodily pain passes like a bird's flight
Into that ice-cold anguish called the grave.
We must accept the trauma of the night.

Beauty is brief, not art; we may ignite
A phoenix fire with a burning stave.
Rave not against the dying of the light.

The miracles of birth and death have height
And depth that we can never hope to brave.
We must accept the trauma of the night.

Drink the sun's blood when it is clear and bright,
Embalm your limbs in a wind-feathered wave.
Rave not against the dying of the light:
We must accept the trauma of the night.

Galatea

for Muriel Spark

Nereid, daughter of the Old Man of the Sea,
How you disliked the bear or elephant
Arriving every day in rustic panoply
From your Cyclopean love-sick suppliant.

Here we see you in your brave nudity,
Your dark-red cloak wind-lifted, fluttering, elegant.
From your twin-dolphin chariot you turn ear and eye
Towards the love-song of the stricken giant.

All movement in this vivacious, classic scene,
Built up with studied and consummate art,
Relates to you. Rough tritons in sea-green

Disport with nymphs and play their amorous part,
Piping and singing in a joyous paean,
While each winged Cupid deftly aims his dart.

Nature Study

My middle-aged eyes fix on the eastern side
In Portland stone of Robert Adam's square, peering
Through elaborate twists of ash-blonde hair
Crown of a body lithe as a young girl's,
A wife filched furtively for a few hours
From a dear friend.
                 Distracted from detachment I can feel
The spasm working up again as her deft fingers
Move across my pubic hair sending sharp shocks
Of beating blood through my receptive phallus.
Too hot we thrust the counterpane aside
And rise together like two homing pigeons
Destined to drop on their own shit-bespattered ledges.
After a pause and preening of feathers
The billing and cooing start up afresh
And only cease when the great square is lost in floods of night.

Roll Call

Bards of mirth and bards of passion
Our names are not exactly writ in water
But so nearly that it is no matter.
With luck we are awarded a Gold Medal
When we have settled firmly in the saddle;
We walk along the streets a little taller
Seeing ourselves waxworks in a Hall of Fame.
But in this contest there is no compassion,
In a few years our style falls out of fashion
Our effigy is carted to the cellar
And the Establishment provides another name.
Passion and mirth are buried in the earth,
Euterpe hastens to assist at a new birth.

Old Pretender

You change your stance from day to day
Outdoing trimmers like the man of Bray,
Equal of Harold Wilson, could I say?
Concealing truth is your *grand métier*.
You cadge and steal from all and sundry,
The poor, the lame, the halt, the hungry.
Ornament of the English bar
Invested with many a foreign Star,
Galloper Smith of our great era
You see the profits even clearer.
During the recent revolution
Which some say, with help from C.I.A.,
Was largely your invention,
You made a packet from the mines of lead;
Patting the blacks upon the head
You quietly removed their bread:
'Let the dead bury their own dead.'
Smarmy and full of bogus charm
Pretending there is no cause for alarm
You do the human race a deal of harm;
You trip up your best friends, m'lud,
And leave them bogged down in the mud.
You'd sell out your own kith and kin
To save your bloody perishing skin.
Peer of the realm, you think yourself a god,
Which I consider rather odd,
You renegade, you murderer, you sod.

Cornish Sea

Crashing down and receding
Gurgling or rippling out
Hoarse indrawn breath
Or snuffling roars
As wind and current change
Sometimes calmly sometimes
Like a mad starving animal
It raked my pebbled childhood
Stroked me to sleep
Or woke my desires.
Too deep too dangerous
Its undertow for me to swim
It was my second love and came
Before my first, its tides
Governed by the moon
Pale distant mistress.
It was, it is, my sea
And still remains
Welling and swelling
In my salt blood
Salter than I, richer at heart
Stronger in every part.

Tokyo Department Store

Along the Ginza every straight line curves
And taxi-drivers fanned by the Wind of Heaven
Show beauty in imbalance. There inside
Is service-with-a-smile and still more smiles.

Through the hoarse twilight amaranthine lights
Climb up, run down, disintegrate and sigh
While Santa Claus shakes off his cotton snow
And rubs his snub nose roughened by *saké* tears.

Children with bud-red cheeks loll on their mothers' backs
Padded with charm and blink and crease
Their fat doll masks. Fathers with faces fresh
From the foxes of the Shinto shrine pray* golf upstairs.

Busloads of tittering schoolgirls hand to mouth
Herded and flagged around the tinsel rooms
Once heavenly butterflies are now king size
And dwarf to impotence the *bonsai* trees.

Faint through the speaker come infant voices
Chanting 'Hark! The Herald Angels Sing'
Or 'Auld Lang Syne' swung slightly off the beam.
Our night is full of wandering balloons.

The fenestrated walls are ringing in delight
With Merry X'mas [*sic*] in golden characters
And on the tree above revolving doors
Is Father Christmas crucified.

* *Phonologically dubious, but substantially true.*

66

Evening is rich with wine and hissing bows,
Morning with aching heads. Life that once seemed
Immense has shrunk to wondering
If east and west are fertile *inter se*.

Note to 'Ikebana', overleaf

Japanese flower-arrangement has many schools and variations. The kenzan *is a small needle-pointed flower holder.* Shin *is the longest stem,* Soe *the second main branch or stem,* Hikae *the shortest.* Jushi *stems are auxiliaries used to vary the patterns.*

Ikebana

In Japan the tea ceremony and cut flowers,
Broken twigs, bent stems, wired shoots and hours
Of practice, gauge a girl's status. In death
A red camellia or a furled leaf can unsheathe
A living language, crucified on spikes of kenzan
By the obedient and attentive Koko-san
According to the rules elaborated by her teacher.
To handle still life well is first of any lady's aims
And yet the geishas seem to do it even better
Just as they play much more amusing games
With chopsticks, handkerchiefs, scissors, stone and paper.

Shin, Soe and Hikae set out well in line
Measured out carefully in correct proportions
With the appropriate angles and declensions
Can achieve eminent and agreeable contortions;
With touches of wayward Jushi they combine
To make a harmonious twangling twine
In a scroll-patterned Jomon vase-container,
But much depends upon the teacher-trainer;
Placed with great skill on a rope-bound cylinder
The group becomes to the beholder a spell-binder.
Circles of sand and nautilus shell diversified
By criss-crossed piles of black-barked oaken logs
With slender slips of silver birch applied
Will give an effect of natural scenery,
Or the sound of waves tossing massive driftwood
On which the eager acolytes can brood.
The general aim is cool tranquillity,
Elegance combined with neat simplicity.
But a world cataclysm can take place on a prism.

Japanese Gardens

'Not to have seen the great gardens of Japan,'
A friend remarked, 'is to be culturally extinct.'
    Grouped shrubs, tapestries of wells and flower-edged ponds,
Curiously shaped boulders and carefully arranged
    Congeries of grey rocks, hooded stone lanterns,
Give to the initiated eye the splendid sweep
    Of a wide landscape. This is the flat garden
Seen best in the Ryoanji Temple at Kyoto,
    Its low walls enclosing on three sides fifteen
Rocks of varying size set in groups on raked white sand,
    Symbol of a tigress fleeing with her cubs
Chased by a leopard from one haven to another.
    There is not a single tree or shrub in sight
But the trees outside the walls and long distance view
    Serve as a backcloth. The Zen composition
Leads the observer to meditation and blank thoughts.
    Different are the hill gardens with shaped lagoons
A green island in the middle, a neat humped bridge, where
    Kingfishers flash living light across the lake
Bright-billed, gem-like birds pounding their catch upon a stone.

    Gardens wet with innumerable mosses
Gardens with eighty kinds of cherry tree in blossom
    Gardens of azaleas, burning maples,
Plum blossom, yellow blue and purple irises,
    Gardens studiously planned and kept with care,
Monuments of high excellence and variety.
    These gardens constructed to rest mind and eye
Have suffered battles, arson, suicides of lovers.
    Flower of them all the Golden Pavilion
Of Kinkakuji was burned by a crazed acolyte.
    Only the garden remains to testify
To five noble centuries of Shogun artistry
    Destroyed in one day of maniac madness.

To a Sick Girl Across Continents

To reinforce your finger-held sanity
I hail you ill in otherworldly weather,
Let us die-stamp perpetual links; so we

Immobilize our whirligig planet-dance,
Project our regions and sight one another
In latitudes not seizable at a glance.

Children may welcome the guttering of a candle
Or start with fright at shadows, then gather
A microcosm from an old sun-dial.

Eyes blurred by age turn stepping-stones to barriers;
Using up history in a gasp men dwindle
Their fanfares to footfalls of pygmy warriors.

True focus of a moment, the mouth upthrust
To kiss or whisper words of brave invention,
Sums our security, funded upon trust.

We roved the lamp-lit streets in rain, still throwing
Sharpened reflections growing in extension,
Till closer contact set our nerve-lines glowing.

Now your bright lightning, grounded, meets high tension
And leaps back to my cloud to raise my voltage;
Distance accelerates not bars love's portage,
Our earthly cross redeems with new dimension.

The Old Blowing-house

for Eugenio Montale

We were together sunk in a fern hollow
Where a bruised engine-house looked sheer
On to the sea, above us granite boulders
Strewn by giants. A sea of beaten copper
Overlooked by storm-clouds ribbed with blood,
My blood and do you remember a drop of it?

The sun shook there in a fretted ripple
And left a skein for your fancy to hold.
Is your hand still on the silken thread?
If you recall the moment does it glow
With gleam of pyrites or are the adits
Of our deep youth grown over? Now
I am alone and breathe an older dark.

Miners with candles at their heads
Probed dripping galleries under the sea
For tin and coughed out their lungs. You freshen
Another air free of the Wolf lighthouse
Spurting as cruelly as a wrecker's flare
In fearful monotonous intervals
Across the bulwark of Castle Kenidjack.

The compass needle trembles inanely
And the weather-cock teeters in the wind
The wind, the pitiless Atlantic gale
Bends dwarf oaks into heaving arches and loosens
A stone from the engine stack that clattering
Rolls down to wound the gathering sea.

After the hurricane comes no clarity.
The pattern gradually blurs and fades
Withering like the flowers on an old quilt.
The sharp curves of images flatten

Recede and vanish into a rubbish heap.
I have lost my land, lying castaway
On sand counted out and outnumbered.

3   *Interlude*

The Mugger

The mugger swims in India's sluggish streams
Dirty deltas and land-locked lakes or basks in sunny dreams
On half-submerged sandbanks or in alluvial mud
Looking much like a floating log or rotting piece of wood.
Displayed in an awesome smiling gape his numerous
Sharp interlocking teeth are vilely venomous
And often used for snatching and devouring those
Who tread by accident upon his toes.
When he is lying idly in the river
His guileful tactics make his victims shiver;
He only shows his slender snout and beady eyes
Ready to take completely by surprise
Some somnolent unwary bird or beast
And turn it into a Lucullan feast.
They never can escape his armoured jaws
As rapidly propelled as buzzing saws
By powerful strokes of his enormous flattened tail
Which whips the water like an animated flail.
He won't come sneakingly behind your back
Catching you roughly by the throat and neck
To rob you of your wallet, purse or hat,
He's much too old and civilized for that;
But he may snap off hand or leg or arm
And do you grievous bodily harm
If you offend his ancient sensibilities and cause alarm
By presuming too much on his native crocodilian charm.

Eating People is Wrong

Human beings are congruously unlike.
Black, yellow, pinko-grey, prognathous,
Pyknic, svelte. Dogs are incongruously similar.
Man-bred dogs that is. The concept Dog
Is becoming almost grotesque. Miniature, mammoth;
Pug-nosed, drooling, asthmatic; hairless, woolly,
Rug-wug, feathered; plantigrade dancer, holy roller.
But dogs exercise their loves and defecations
Publicly and proudly. Humans in secret,
And often with embarrassment. Dogs fawn,
Slobber and sentimentalize because we
Have corrupted them. Yet one fine difference
Still remains. According to Fleet Street
They have improved on our ethic. Dog don't eat dog.

Computer-wise

Long years ago man thought he had to find
Within himself the way where he was going.
It turns out that he was completely wrong.
Now he employs a gimmick of a kind
That answers if he gives the right address.
What he feeds in is what he has in mind.
What he gets out is anybody's guess.

The trouble is the thing might go berserk and come unstuck,
Punch an unwanted hole, miss its intended goal
And lose a vital trick, causing a cosmic crunch.
This really would be rotten luck on blokes like us
Who've worked so bloody hard to make the gadget tick,
And all the time I'm haunted by a horrid hunch
That if it does there'll be an astronomic mess.

The Fall of Phaëthon

for Derek Parker

Youth of divine birth and limited intelligence,
He begged his father a disastrous favour.
The god consenting swore by Styx in self-defence
And Phaëthon, put on his best behaviour,
Went off to drive the sun's great chariot for one day.
Lacking the god's firm hand the horses bolted right away,
Came too near the earth, dried rivers, made the soil decay.
The universe would have been destroyed by fire
Had Zeus not intervened with Olympian ire
And struck with lightning force the foolish clown,
Sending him crashing through the air to drown
In the deep Eridanus. There his sisters dear,
The Heliads, came to his tomb to shed a tear.
For this kind gesture they were cruelly turned
To poplar trees, weeping amber drops that burned.

This dramatic scene has frequently been painted.
A lady looking at the picture nearly fainted:
'I don't quite get,' she said, 'the gist of this event,
But there seems to have been a nasty accident.'

Cosmetics

Don't overdo the decoration pet
Or else you'll end, like Kitty Fisher, dead:
The bloody stuff is full of lethal lead.
Never for one minute let yourself forget
Even in moments of your greatest pride
That beauties rarely get beatified.

Fibi Pronounced Phoebe

I considered a cat
But she looked like a dog;
Some suggested a bat,
I considered a cat.
She was certainly fat
And resembled a hog.
I considered a cat
But she looked like a dog.

Morning

M'illumino
d'immenso
'I illuminate myself with immensity'
The poet remarked with great intensity.
'Those who can't understand the miracle of density
For which I have a strong propensity
Are simply persons of insane insensity.'

Sunday Ads

OXFAM *needs money*
for two physiotherapists
to work on leprosy in India
et avec les fraises des bois
CHARTREUSE
Top left-hand, top right-hand,
Nicely balanced, prettily poised,
Or, perhaps, a little precariously.
Anyhow, a sign of the times.
But whose mouth are you watering?
Whose skin are you saving?

The Ballad of a Sad Decay

As I walked down our country lane
    Everything was groovy;
The flowers began to escalate
    Like a Kubrick movie,

They suffer from dyslexia
    Having no words to speak
While acid anorexia
    Makes my stomach squeak.

I listened to the weeny-boppers' scream
    Pierce the polluted air;
Hearing them burst their bubble-gummed-up dream
    I wished I wasn't there.

Local yokels move like yo-yos
    With Muzak in their ears,
Tatty barmaids goof like go-gos
    The mystique of the years.

I handed in my Barclaycard
    To buy a glass of stout
But owing to an escarpade
    My credit had run out.

The critics knocked my book of pomes
    In the new *Fab Bookay*
Because they thought the Zurich gnomes
    Had ground my heart away.

Although I'm crazy like a fox
    I try to keep my cool
And fiddle with the goggle-box
    For fear I look a fool.

It's useless to chat up the boys
  I'm not an agitprop,
They make a lot of concrete noise
  Which looks to me like cock.

I'd like to sink in a think-tank
  But I am getting square,
I'm skint, I only drink red plonk,
  Balding, with grotty hair.

There's little left for tired old mugs
  Except to train as muggers.
Have mercy Lord on bugs and thugs
  And us poor hijacked buggers.

Notes

COSMETICS—*Kitty Fisher (1740?–1767) the actress, who sat three times for Reynolds, died from an excessive use of cosmetics.*
FIBI PRONOUNCED PHOEBE—*The rhymes are those listed in the Concise Oxford Dictionary.*
MORNING—*Giuseppe Ungaretti's (1888–1970) famous hermetic poem 'Mattina' was written on 26th January 1917 at Santa Maria La Longa when he was a soldier at the front. Having given varying explanations of the poem in his earlier years, Ungaretti became rather fretful when asked to explain it in his old age.*

4 *Daybook*

Futile Defences

After the expected flattering speeches
And the unexpectedly leaden handshake
The delectable twining of limbs in the
Secret attic room almost forgotten
He retired just outside the commuting area
To cultivate his garden and surround it
With a wall of dark discouragement
Ostensibly to blunt time's slings and fortune's arrows
And the darts of common hate or love.

He did not know that hurt or joy might fall
From the sky like the sting of a thwarted bee
Or the riddling rays of the sun. Nor did he care.
Nothing had meaning, not even the M.B.E.
Which he had kept and treasured so long in its
Black leather case in the worm-eaten writing desk.

He did not hear or see the passing world but lay
Inert like a tin god toppled from his pedestal
Gathering slow slime in a disused fountain.

Birdscape

for Henry Donner

At daybreak a throng of finches animate
The leaves of the huge still bay tree, *laurus*
Nobilis of the Romans, with a flutter
Of rustling twitters they begin to unfold
Their dawn chorus. With winged social instincts
They discuss the morning and perhaps us. The tree
Is a cloud of unknowing among incessant
Woodwind blowing chirps and trills. Loudly.
Unintelligible tattle in a maze of boughs.

They and their tree are us as we are
Them, sired by earth, sea and air. Bud-pickers
Fruit-peckers, seed-eaters they take off
On their dipped undulating flights pink-polled
Sage-green, yellow and black, red-breasted.
Skied over them small dun-coloured
Terrestrial birds sing complicated rising
Melodies jumping thirds and sixths. Somewhere
In the air currents below, the faithful swallows
Reconnoitre, swoop, seize and recover,
The rising sun glistening their plumage.

Swallows, it is well that you migrate
On sidelong wings into a fiercer sun.
To homeling birds, blithe harmless singers,
Will come darkening autumnal afternoons
And the minatory sound of distant gunshot.

In the unsealing light we dumb discover
Ourselves under a lichened stone awaiting
The moment of wakening unknown music.

Alexandrian Profile

for Enrique de Rivas

The poet who stood at a slight angle
To the universe saw and suffered more
Than the vertical man whom we no longer
Honour, more than the horizontal man,
Strangely deformed by automatic coupling,
Who serves the casual cunts of willing wives.

Cavafy conquered the eroding sin of guilt.
He knew that when we are born we are not done for.
He entered the minds of barbarians
And emperors and the bodies of boys.
What he saw was desire in a squalid alley,
What he suffered was the piercing root of love.

To him the lovely limbs and lips he found
On a secret mattress in a clandestine room
Were some kind of a solution.
The touch of a hand, the smell of a handkerchief
Became poetry in a month or in a year.
The mirror of his mind held the beauty
Of a handsome boy until it flowered into verse.

With an elegant convoluted sentence
Left hanging half finished in the sluggish
Mediterranean air, he sculptured
A dignified, classical response
To the green pain of his remembered pleasure.

Undersong

I am speaking into a tube
Into the suffocating, rumbling
Underground of sound
Beating upwards in feud
Against the blue air which once
Humbling and silencing words
Surrounded me with the gift
Of converse with small birds.

But wait. The birds are here too,
Their wings brushing the russet roofs.
The Roman *rondini*
Chattering their high-pitched song.

Jamie

(born 19th May 1963, died 3rd August 1967)

Keelhauled we cry out, 'Someone is missing!'
There is a hole within our heads and hearts
That no caulking can stop up or fill.
The house is cobwebbed by our memories
Of him and all his dogged braveries.

People were walking to and fro
On the Vittorio Veneto
When we went there ten years ago
To show it to our foreign friends.
He came to us at midnight
Hawked with his brother
By a small boy with dirty hands
In the effervescent light.
What breed he was we did not know,
This handful of sable and white
With vivid button eyes,
Diminutive in size.

This Lilliputian dog when fully grown
Emerged as an aristocrat
From the tip of his black foxy nose
To the end of his fine feathered tail,
A miniature volpino,
The carriage dog that sat
Beside the Bourbon kings and queens.

His coat was shining silk, a golden red
Down his neat spine, shading to delicate cream
Beneath, a noble ruff across his chest.
His legs were sleek and russet-coloured
With pale gold feathering at the back,
But born as he was in a Roman shack
Four infant weeks of worms and rickets

Had faintly dimmed his harrowing beauty.

At first he was too tiny to climb stairs
And made his journeys with grand airs
In the pocket of Margot's patterned apron.
His favourite resting place was on
The lowest basket of the vegetable stand
Which kept him safely within bounds
Curled in cacophonies of kitchen sounds
And sniffing savoury odours.

The garden in those days
Was a wilderness of weeds
Some six feet high.
Between the fruit-trees
And the tall grass
Jamie would play
A quicksilver game of 'I spy'
Or hide and seek,
Bobbing and weaving round the hose
Like a fly-weight boxer on his toes.

Jamie was his mistress's shadow dog.
When she was ill or indisposed
Nothing could tempt him from her side.
Anyone who interposed
Even to give him food
Would get a nasty nip
From his sharp fox-like teeth.

He knew instinctively
The people whom we did not trust
And those who had no right of entry.
The first he treated with disgust
Barely concealed, against the rest
He defended with infinite zest
Our rural property.

After the clammy winter and the wild wet spring
The summer heat was suffocating.
But in the mellow autumn days
We had the *ottobrate* of the Alban Hills,
And life with Jamie was a hymn of praise,
A growing, crowning joy.

When he was happy, hungry or inquisitive,
He would dance round and round like a small top,
His front legs signalling,
Paws waving in the air in urgent prayer,
Demanding a biscuit or a passing cat.
Thwarted in this last request
He ran off nimbly in a vain pursuit.
Of the three dogs he was the leader and the king;
They followed him, he taught them everything.

Our ancient house had been unoccupied,
Except for families of filthy squatters,
For twenty years or more. The local boys,
Liars and thieves, the sons of thieves and liars,
Scaled the high walls and stole our fruit.
Jamie hated these young plunderers
With their delinquent ways
And so his courage was his own undoing.
One morning the two other dogs came back
Trembling into the sitting-room.
But Jamie failed to come.

I called him and I called. In vain.
His small limp body free from pain
Lay at the bottom of the water tank.
Fearlessly he had stood his ground upon the bank
Against the boys,
And they had shot him dead
Between the eyes
With a lead pellet from a catapult.
The frightened pair had fled.

Now he lies wrapped in flowers beneath the ground,
His burning loyalty unquenched on earth,
His constant bravery confirmed.
Jamie, you have gone to a new-found land,
Secure from vile terrestial danger,
With nobler vistas and a greener garden.

Bruckner at the Royal Albert Hall

A burst of spontaneous sound from the young in the arena
    Breaks the smothered atmosphere; a kind of VIVAT
Hailing the first violin and inviting the conductor
    To take his place on the podium and begin.
The musicians in their Red Sea rig would have pleased neither
    The Austrian composer nor Prince Albert, but the
Mysterious string figures and the rising, rousing trumpet theme
    Heard by fourteen thousand ears brings them both back
To thrilling life. As the music unfolds, it shapes itself
    Into an edifice round, arched and repetitive
Like this Victorian Hall. The peasant organist and the
    Consort prince unite with the return of trumpets
And heavy majestic brass, melting and fusing together
    With building and audience in the echoing air.

Rome Sweet Rome

Night or day, wet or fine, hail or snow, cloud or stars,
I'm racked by the animal roars of Roman motor-cars
And the loud curses of the insane Roman motorist.
W. S. Gilbert should have put them on his list,
None of the bastards ever would be missed.
What shall I do to stop this hideous noise?
Batten down the shutters, turn on the electric light,
Prepare myself for one more day of night?
Take out my paint-box and my childhood toys,
Play solitaire, one-handed whist or invent other ploys?
Read Roget's *Thesaurus* and the dictionary through
Until I anaesthetize myself against this hullabaloo?

Harvests

He who sowed the dragon's teeth
And reaped armed men,
Sowed with a stone dissension
And blows and bitter death.

You who followed Echo's voice,
'Come! Come!' gazed in the pool
And could not rise
Held by a face so beautiful.

Rejoicing in the fluid mirror
You killed yourself with self-sown grief,
But from you sprang the white flower
With blood-red heart and fresh green leaf.

Fear Question

'If you fear God,' said the prophet Gadhafi,
'You cannot fear anything else.'
But many God-fearing men
Fear the Black September murderers,
The new men of Munich.
'What do you mean by fear, Colonel Gadhafi?'
May God forgive you; the circle is closed.

Credo of a Stick-in-the-Mud

for Kenneth Clark

I prefer order to chaos
Urbino's gracious hill to Laos.
I prefer creation to destruction
The Garden of Eden to eruption
And light to gelignite.
I prefer gentleness to violence
A soft answer to an electric fence.
I prefer forgiveness to vendetta
Mercy to a shot from a Beretta.
I prefer courtesy to rudeness
Talleyrand's charm to Mintoff's crudeness.

All living things are linked together
In unity, as sister is to brother,
And we must learn to tolerate each other.
I believe in those great works of thought and art
That stimulate the mind and touch the heart,
The music of humanity that's near to tears
And the celestial harmony that moves the spheres.

The North Cliffs

We went off to the North Cliffs
Early on a pale spring morning
And the sea glinted grey.
On the heather at one side
Of the rough steep path winding
Down for three hundred feet
Were the rusty remains of an old bicycle,
Chain, mudguards, a broken lamp.
The handlebars and saddle
Mingled into a bull's head.
On the other side were a brassiere
And a pair of ripped nylon pants.
The girl must have put up a tough fight.

Mourning for Michelangelo

Eliot wrote of women who come and go
Talking of Michelangelo. Now they would cease
And join with us to mourn a bitter blow.
Today a man came, but not to walk in peace;
With a small hammer he destroyed a masterpiece.
The holy group carved from a flawless block
Of clear Carrara marble for a cardinal
By Michelangelo's young hand, firm as a rock,
Is lost forever to us all; a battered symbol
Like a broken ampersand, an and which is no and,
A pietà with a fine beginning and a shattered end.
Shouting 'I am Christ!' the Australian profaner
Desecrated his own image and, insaner,
Murdered the immortal body of his mother.

Rome, 21st May 1972

Venus in Transit

for George Fraser

I was driving fast along the rocky
Wooded mountainside of shallow slow Ardèche
When I saw three teenage girls fresh from the
River sitting on a hump of tufted grass.
The middle one, a blonde between brunettes,
With beautifully free-slung breasts and long lithe
Sun-tanned thighs, stretched her waving round arms out
To enfold me
Or so it seemed then on that hot summer day.

Such things happen when I cannot stop and
Gather them in, but the gesture and the image
Remain, more lively, doubly felt because
Unthinkable, near but unattainable,
Continuing unbroken and forever
Unfinished, unimpaired by attitude or
The faintest semblance of physical act
To enfold her
However apposite and satisfying.

Venus so often unobserved chooses
Her ravishing, cold, star-racked appearances
With mantic, rare and more than mortal skill.

Simple Song

When the bracken is rusty
And the stubble is yellow
I'll follow a fellow
As long as he's trusty.

When the ash-tree is leafing
And the oak is in bud
I'll spill his young blood
If he leaves my heart grieving.

The Arrangeable Dog

Fibi of whom you have already heard
In a triolet, is no blooming violet.
Elderly but cunning as a cuckoo bird
She can lay herself in someone else's nest
Or sink gracefully into her own, at request
Or as circumstances dictate. A very
Arrangeable dog, amenable to every
Kind of approach and smart as an equerry.
You can curl her up in the corner or
Stretch her flatways alongside the mirror.
Hospitable too she rises from her nest
And gravely warpling greets each honoured guest.
Striking is her peculiar liking for leaning
Against a shelf of reference books when sleeping.
She always fits into any cubic place
According to Parkinstein's law of expanding space.
A diminishing return is not her concern.
Such a tractable dog with a charming face.

Note

Warpling *is a combination of* warp *and* wiggling. *It is achieved by a spinning move-ment when balanced on one haunch.*

How to Achieve Peace

Peace is an ancient word implying quiet
But now it is more likely to include a riot.
To achieve peace it is thought necessary
For rockets, shell and missiles to miscarry
And fall on boys and girls and pregnant mothers;
This is officially known as 'encouraging the others'.
Dropping napalm on allied troops and friends
Is one more move to further peaceful ends.
Sending letter-bombs by international mail
Makes us feel confident, secure and hale.
Famine, rapine and rape are assets to the cause
Like opium, morphine and undeclared wars.
All keep the home fires burning, spread good cheer
And militate towards a peaceful atmosphere.
A canny Roman summed it up, I guess:
'They make a wilderness and call it peace.'

William Empson

A genial man, perhaps a genius,
I often met him in our Cambridge days.
Together we appeared in 1929
Sine and cosine
In an anthology of poetry,
I with nine stilted lines
Never reprinted, he
With six masterpieces almost beyond praise.

Betrayed by the head porter, ostracized by dons,
Missing the pros, he was sentenced by the cons,
A lamentable case of academic *mores*
Prompted by puritan envy and trumped-up stories.

Later, during my holidays from Helsinki
I saw him at his Marchmont Street abode,
Hands always inky.
One entered skating on a kipper bone
And heavily collapsed on a commode
Garnished with scraps of egg and bacon.
Refreshed by tepid beer
Served in smeared tooth glasses
One settled down to hear
The youthful sage spinning his paradoxes.

Paul Dirac reached full maturity
When twenty-six, William Empson
Had behind him a fine score
Of poems and *Seven Types of Ambiguity*
At twenty-four.
Dirac alas did little more
But William's genius tenaciously went on.

In Tokyo, teaching at the Bunrika Daigaku,

He became a National Treasure.
His Japanese students were trying to construe
In other words and at their leisure
A few well-known English proverbs:
'Out of sight, out of mind', became
'Invisible, insane.'

Learning to paint with Mrs Nishiwaki's aid
He made a splendid start
But put more pigment on suit and carpet
(Here Lady Sansom cannot be gainsaid)
Than on the canvas, which baulked his art.
He rode to work on a whisky diet
And had his love-play with the parlour-maid
Of the somewhat sinister Swiss Minister.
Ski-ing down the mountain he could not brake
When nearing a precipice
But God and Richard Brown were there
And William didn't turn a hair.

In Singapore we lurched and searched
Among the sailors in every sleazy den
For Nobby Clark, but the man
We found was not his Nobby
Much to his chagrin.
He didn't know, who chose words as his hobby,
That in the Navy Clarks are all called Nobby.

Cracked up to the skies by Margaret and me
We had arranged next day
For him to burgeon
At a literary luncheon.
The ladies, dressed in the most stylish way,
Looked at him in awe.
Before the food appeared the poet stood.
An opening speech? Yes, short and quick:
'I'm going out to be sick.'
And that was all the ladies heard or saw.

During the China Incident
Came the long trek
By the exiled Peking universities,
Of which he was a teaching member;
So William went
To Hunan and Yunnan.
He ran about in hope, on trust,
Happy to have escaped from the pell-mell.
The teachers taught just
What they could remember
In strict rotation,
Having no way to check.
This suited William well,
He being a master of misquotation.

In London he brought handsome Hetta
To lunch with us at the Café Royal,
Their first time out together,
He married her for worse or better,
Always loyal.

Able to move from Wonderland to Milton's God
From Folly to Sense and Sensibility,
From Mesopotamia to the English Dog,
Blinking like a Wykehamist hooded owl
Through thick glasses at something odd,
Our William has no peer
In providing meat for the critical soul
Making the difficult look easy
Sighting a new variant or a fence to clear
Or finding some lost cause to cheer.

What I admire most about you, William, I,
Is your indifference to the habits
And conventions of society;
Men should walk and talk like men,
Not hobbits or rabbits,
And likewise women;

By all of which I mean your truth to your own I
And your unalterable honesty.

A Warning to Jeerleaders

for John Gifford

The blind are most respected
    And led from here to there,
The deaf are just neglected
    Or jeered from there to here.

    Deaf to the world
    I lip-read what I think
    In the mirror as I shave—
    And shrink.

The Eyes Don't Always Have It

Freud sat with his back
To his patients to prevent
Contact of eye with eye.
Otherwise such an event
Might have produced an inward crack.
We have always, we timid ones,
Feeling it in our bones,
Hesitated to speak,
To make a break.
We have avoided the enquiring eye
The censorious eye
The cold analytical eye.
An eye can be
An intimidating enemy
Or a doting and dangerous friend.
Either could lead to a sticky end.
What we aloof people need
To be freed
Is a quiet and companionable void,
Quite unlike Freud.

Roman Elections

In ancient Rome when tribunes were elected
The occasion was serious and solemn,
Even though there were riots and armed conflict
In the streets when Tiberius Gracchus fell.
The ceremonies and the voting urns
Were honoured and respected by the plebs
And the patricians, at least in earlier days.

In Rome today elections are a cross between
A fair-ground, vaudeville and cabaret,
With a slight touch of Grand Guignol thrown in.
The Neo-Fascists and the Communists perform
Intricate manœuvres, the Royalists are mute,
The Christian Democrats repeat themselves.
One almost might expect Big Wheels, Cake Walks,
Great Dippers, Giant Strides and Mystery Trains,
As well as bread and circuses.

Along the streets shaded by high palaces,
Their noble names, Borghese, Barberini,
Ruspoli, Colonna and Orsini
Unknown to the ignorant and illiterate
Emigrants from the Abruzzi and the South
Who arrogantly assume the status
Of Roman citizens, horns hoot, brakes scream,
Cars rev up, pedestrians leap wildly in the air.

Youthful demonstrators stroll languidly
In mezzo alla strada, blocking up
The traffic, normally nearly static,
For hours and hours, while ambulances
And police cars sweep through. Tons of paper
Leaflets are scattered, blow about and grow
Mushy under the tread of rain-soaked feet,

Propaganda from the nine principal parties
Embellished by photographs of senators
And deputies. Banners with shields and slogans
Are slung festooned across the thoroughfares,
Popular tunes blurt out in blasts from radios
Carried by garlanded vans, loud hailers howl.
Noise, dust, confusion, filth and anarchy.

At night flood-lights illuminate the monuments
Of old and modern times, the Wedding Cake,
The Capitol, a masterwork of Michelangelo,
And the russet ruins of the Palatine.
The unsuspecting tourists stare and gape
At places where the augurs sought the omens.
They think that Rome is still inhabited by Romans.

Deus in Machina

I was dozing on my balcony in urban shade
When I saw the outriders of a motor cavalcade
Escorting with great pomp some King or Head of State to greet
The Italian President at his Quirinal seat.

Traffic was held up for a minute to the indignation
Of Roman drivers who thought the visit an abomination
A direct insult to their Roman pride, rage and disgust
Filled their thoughts, usually occupied by push and thrust.

Romans are married to their cars, they are their flesh and blood,
Their love for them is fiercer than their love of fatherhood;
Part of their being they are the symbol of virility
And woe to him who challenges this even with civility.

Just like the Roman motorbicyclist, I realized,
The modern Roman motorist is a centaur mechanized.

In Memory of Risepark Geham Grey Cloud

Cloudy, our Schnauzer, did not take to Schnapps,
(With deference to George MacBeth)
But met his miserable death
When left in the dissembling laps
Of a sweet man, a former priest,
And his dear homely wife,
Or so they seemed, to say the least,
Until they eased him out of life.
The man, too good to make a friar,
Turned out to be an awful liar.
Between them they did Cloudy in,
Which some might deem a mortal sin.
Consumed by guilt or fright
They never told us of that night
When our poor timid pet
Was taken to the vet,
But daring only to deceive
They said that he was happy and alive.
Now we are left to grieve
And keep his memory bright.

Rightness is All

A million dead fish floating on the Rhine
To make our dirty linen clean and fine;
Countries destroyed to save them from their fate
Ostensibly from love and not through hate;
Risking men's lives to pick up bits of rock
And prove superior to the Soviet bloc;
Trapping rare animals to make fur coats
As gifts to young girls from randy old goats;
Ancient and lovely buildings razed to rubble
So that traffic, trade and tourism can double;
Spraying with chemicals the vegetation
To ruin the digestion of a nation;
Abandoning social life to watch the telly
And atrophying brain to fill the belly;
Committing arson, setting fire to trees,
Murdering birds, small animals and bees,
To free protected land and make a building site;
Surely so many wrongs must make a right?

Henry Moore at Forte di Belvedere

(*20th May 1972*)

Under the high patronage of President and Queen
Silently observing the overcrowded scene
He who made Queens and Kings from excrement
Of earth, from wood and stone and metals,
Fantastic flowers with variegated petals,
Reveals to us the sum of his long life's achievement
Flood-lit at evening with an unearthly sheen
Against the magic background of a medieval screen.

The Princess opens the event in Florentine half-light:
We are exposed to figures static and moribund,
Atavistic in their ancient aboriginality.
Man has returned to his primeval night
Dreaming the uneasy dreams of the cave-bound.
Form is tied to form with strings as light as day
That only Orpheus on his lute can play.
Affirmation is opposed to doubt and ambiguity.

Heads appear as stumps, vital parts have holes,
Bodies are embryonic, impersonal, remote,
Far from the world of High Renaissance wholes.
This turning from the classic modes is a stern antidote
To facile realizations of the natural world
And the romantic rocks on which slave ships are hurled.
Moore's deep-rooted common sense of wrong and right
Is matched by his uncommon power of inward sight.

In the late Thirties there suddenly appear
Jumbling mechanical objects prophesying war.
The cataclysm when it came drove families
Underground; Moore followed them with wakeful eyes
And drew their huddled forms and bundled frames,
Grey ghostly figures haunted by the sound of trains,
A paraphrase of the living dead and a dissection

Of people swathed like Lazarus before his resurrection.

Art is to Moore a universal thing, activity
Linking past and present in its continuity,
Dismemberment is a preliminary to rebirth.
Delving he searches for reality in the cave
From which his stone is dug and from the earth
Wherein his elmwood starts its growth from seedling grave
To the broad statement springing stave by stave
Until it reaches the plainsong of full maturity.

Norma

Through the long elegant apartment
With a balcony overlooking San Carlino
She moves insulated and tranquil
Among the T'ang figures and Sung vases
Oblivious of Piranesi's Views of Rome.
Venice to her
Might be the capital of Vietnam.

Beaten from birth by father, grandmother,
Stepfather and mother-in-law, beaten
On her wedding day, beaten into
Impassivity, beaten
She watched her young husband,
A bricklayer who only worked
Two years in twelve,
Dying of cancer. Plugged with morphia
He rose in his bed, cursed her
And hit her in the face.
It was his last living act.

Small, dainty, beautiful, with raven hair,
Her unlined face smiles rarely,
It is too concerned with difficult duties,
With laying knives and forks
In English style,
Waiting at table in bib and tucker
And serving me tea in my pyjamas.
She does not know the names of the streets
Next to where she lives. She is
Beyond knowledge, wrapped
In insensibility
And beyond hope, an automaton
Staggering fashionably along
In a short blue dress on platform soles.

Bereft of relatives and friends
She lives in a leaking, bare, unheated garret
Where her two children,
A girl of eleven and a boy of ten
One clever and fetching, the other
Stupid and disobedient,
Weigh on her strangled heart and muted mind.
A widow of twenty-seven
Who looks eighteen,
Forced to embroider ten dull hours a day
For a pittance that her husband took
And frittered uselessly away,
Sickened by touch of men,
Reduced to impotence,
She cannot speak out.
Impossible to tell what makes her tick
Or even if anything goes on
Behind her sage-green eyes and tiny breasts.

General Paralysis of the Sane

Our time is sprained
Dislocated and spavined,
Seconds are spilled
And minutes fractured,
Hours are tolled
By funeral bells
From a variety of hells.

At night, by day, in sun and rain
Men, women and children
Torture, shoot and destroy
Men, women and children
Everywhere and whenever.
Jungle mud writhes
With severed limbs
Punctured by hypodermics.
Down the next street,
In the next state,
They are looting houses
Of friend and foe.
The air is dense with beautiful bricks
And fragments of stained glass.

Over there a petrol bomb or a grenade
Or CS gas, nearer at hand
Pale faces pressed against window-panes
Hear a volley of rubber bullets
And the crash of a classical cupola.
What does one more matter?

Rabbit-like we stand paralysed
By the serpent's crooked smile.
We look and listen
Rent, spent and silent.

What man, beast, insect or machine
Is coming after us
To repair and repay
Our near-irreparable loss
And make straight the way
That has been torn and bent?

Seven Up

for C. P. Snow

The ideal city is laid up in heaven
But here on earth we have a mystic seven.
The seven deadly sins, the seven
Virtues and the seven works of mercy, the seven
Branches of the candlestick, the seven
Stages of the Cross, the seven
Last words of Christ, the seven
Joys of Mary and her seven
Sorrows, the seven churches of Asia, the seven
Bishops and the seven deacons, the seven
Wonders of the world and the seven
Champions of Christendom, the seven
Against Thebes, the seven gods of luck, the seven
Samurai, the seven sleepers in their cave, the seven
Sages of Greece, the tales of the Seven
Wise Masters, the seven seas, the seven
Heavens, the seven stars and seven planets, the seven
Hills of Rome, Seven Dials and the Seven
Years War, the seven senses of the soul, the seven
Sacraments of the Church, the seven
Angels of the Apocalypse with their seven
Trumpets and seven plagues and seven
Bowls and seven seals and seven
Vials of wrath, Salome's dance of the seven
Veils, the seven gifts of the Holy Church, the seven
Sciences, the seven days of the week, the seven
Daughters of the priest of Midian and Bilhah's seven
Sons, Dowland's Lachrymae or Seven
Teares figured in seven
Passionate Pavans, the seven
Ages of man, Wordsworth's We Are Seven,
The Seven Sisters and Kivi's Seven Brothers.
The symbolic number seven excels all others.

Fibi Fading

Born into the misery of a Genzano garage
Twelve months drenched black with oil
We found her under a Volvo of some age.
A murmuring heart was her sad heritage.
After a few baths her matted hair curled
To a light chestnut and she entered our garden world.
Fibi was a quick learner and always had something to say.
She is dying now in a dignified way.
Her old head nods to and fro in a coil
Of thought, and reverently up and down.
She is clever, nobody's fool, still a bit of a clown.
With supreme concentration she can look at me
Clearly and steadily, with an unswerving eye
But what she is thinking is a private mystery.
She knows that we know she is dying
And that there is no use crying
But she will never show it. All goes on as before
Except that she cannot sometimes explore
The wherefore and the why.
Waterlogged she can hardly waddle
Who once braved mounting seas to paddle.
She will not bark at intruders again
Or chase cats to their bolt-holes down the drain.
She will not see her imaginary portrait
Painted in oils, revealing every trait
Of her delightful character, which has been
Commissioned in England, a country far away
That she has heard of but never seen.
She eats almost nothing but politely acknowledges
The plates set out for her in her favourite places.
She drinks a little water, trembles and shakes
And extends in the air one paw bent with aches.
She is saying goodbye in her own way.

Trick Cyclist

I throw out my arms to grasp
And contain your contour
But you escape my span whoever
Or wherever or whatever you are,
It, id, king, beggar-maid,
Sagittarius, Capricorn,
Old man or thistle, widow or weed,
Bird, beast, insect, reptile or fish.
There must be a point
Of contact, tenuous perhaps
As a spider's web. But where?
Among trees? Along the sand?
In little holes? Up in the sky?
Through swamps? Down in the sea? But when?
Immeasurable ghost
I will pursue you on my bicycle
Through boughs, along beaches, into the ground,
Up in the air, across mud, down in the depths,
Among the constellations,
Until there are no more years.

Fibi's Last Verse

She died lovingly, with a last lick, grateful
For her release from hateful
Maladies, but I still see her
Round every corner, under every chair.
I feel her rubbing against my leg
At dinner as when she used to beg.
Painfully, but appropriately, she left
Her last message on the Feraghan carpet,
Marking it unfadingly on warp and weft
With a blood-range stain and discharged her debt.

Aubade

My worldswept wife
My trouble and strife
Born in Mayfair,
Who can imitate Cockney
As if bred in Hockney,
You are my despair.
Once bonny and hale
The girl for a gale
Tough, unafraid
A *jolie-laide*,
You are now skin and bone
Beyond my aid.
Powerless as a stone
I cannot atone
For what I have done.

The alarm-clock spell
Sounds its warning knell.
You have to get up
In the morning murk
Swig down a quick cup
And go off to work.
How wearing
It is, and tearing,
And how well you know it,
To be wife to a poet.

Indian Summer

for Alan Ross

At a perfect curve in the line
Of my irregular life
The maple trees flared in me
Like bursts of shrapnel.
Such miraculous conjunctions
Of heavenly moments
Breaking over me like waves
Happen too rarely
In these shortening autumn days.

Dearest

Shreds of memory hang from the picked bones
Of her small body shrivelled by age
And illness to a question mark,
Past mixes confusedly with the non-present
Both dying in a whispered breath.
She lived long on the point of a needling pain
But what we remember is her gaiety
Her grasp of life and the love she permeated
Through young and old, rich and poor, bankers, butchers,
Milliners, barrow-boys and garbage collectors
Until everything glowed and was alight with her being.

Nightcap

I hammer on my head until I see
A friend or enemy of poetry.
I lift the cap that covers my brain hole
Admit the friend and chase away the ghoul.

Daily I sweat and halt and jog slowly on,
At night wings speed me like Bellerophon.
My myth is weak, O Lord, so strengthen me
Against the snares and wiles of Hobbitry.

Pathos of mortal things strikes at my heart
But suffering itself cannot build art.
A springing tiger or a swoop of swallows
May move us more than dead men on the gallows.

On My Sixty-Sixth Birthday

Clickety click said bones. Late winter rain
Fed the spring's marrow, light-tongued summer brought
Singing fruit after eighteen years of drought,
Crickets chirped. Such days may not come again.

Night forged forgotten links into a chain,
Lit fires, dug up old rags and bones and caught
The strands of memory. Battles were fought
And won over hours and years of pain.

The break in my brain was quicker to heal
Than the vile wounds of internecine strife
That harrow the heart-strings of those who feel.

Dumbly I stand and wait for the honed knife
Hoping I may be granted strength to steal
Some healing moment from our stricken life.

Rome, 2nd September 1972

Renascence

To your low, husky voice
Laden with delight,
Softly awakes my art
From the clammed sleep
In which it was encased
Away from joys
Of sound and sight.
Gently it takes great strides
To leap into your heart
And there it hides
Humble and deep
Able to laugh or weep
Play any part
Until you are deceased.

Crowning Mercies

Lovers at least remain happy
Through quarrels and quinsies
And painful pettinesses
Knowing as they do what is thought
Without speech and what is felt
Without thought. Such sympathy
Will outlive the twists of calendars
And last out lifetimes
Of fair and foul weather
However circumstances change
Outward trivial things
And age alter faces and figures.
When everything is forgiven
And expiated between lovers
Even death's worm will not be strange.

5 *Nightlights*

The Ancient Enemies

for Francis King

The outer darkness slakes
    And lightly breaks
     Over the bloody shirt I've worn
The silent fusillade of dawn.

I walk into the breakfast room
    As to a tomb
     And in the coffee lees
Are all the ancient enemies.

I sit and marvel that the wind
    Can sift my mind
     Into a compost heap
Of ragged memories that creep.

Shake spear! Break light!
    The hand in white
     Shall hold the sword
Until I speak the killing word.

Incommunicado

Things have broken and I have a hole
In my head to let in a confusion
Of sound, a Babel of non-soul
As in a tunnel after the collision
Of two trains. Who is dead
And who is alive? Speak, speak!
What language, what was it you said?
My tongue cannot twist itself to break
Into speech or be trusted to utter.
Nothing that enters my head makes sense
And nothing intelligible comes out. A shutter
Has come down over my brain like a fence
Against reason or an immense
Affront to what made me a part
Of humanity and the miracle of art.
All that is left to me is a wandering word
Not understood or not heard.

Unfree Fall

Lost along the corridor
I tried every door.
Each door was locked
And I had lost the keys.
Shocked
Buckled at the knees
Groping in the air
For the treacherous rope
I lost hope.
Down the great marble stair
I fell and fell.
A tripwire I felt
Tearing my ankle
And saw a gloating face above.
There were no more doors
And the keys were lost in unlove.

Chartless

Leaving this territory
I lose the sea
And landmarks
By which I used
To navigate. Arks
Rested here, birds fused
With the air,
Animals marched
Pair by pair.
Now I am clear
Of day and year,
Hungry and parched
Without a compass,
No land, only sky
And weed, at an underpass
To nowhere, a Sargasso sea
In which to lie
And rot and slowly die.

Prisoners' Round

for Anthony Bottrall

We tunnel through the ground to find the light
And when it comes it cuts our eyes like flint.
The knowledge of the light we cannot bear.

If we could only learn to live in shade
Tilling our gardens, leaning on a spade,
We should not need to move into the glare.

It is the light that dazzles. We cannot view
What tree it is that blocks our hate of you,
Great Nobodaddy sitting on a gate.

A gate that leads behind the prison bars
Where light comes faintly homing from the stars;
So we must tunnel once again, and wait.

Darkling No

I lie in prison like a discarded god
Condemned for failure
Senseless but not quite dead.
Chains I endure
While barred shadows over my head
Hit like a rod.
Ichabod!
No rainbows come or go,
What little I can hear or see
Is bounded by a darkling No
Without a hint of immortality.
True dreams come at dawn
When the Ivory Gate changes to Horn.

Outside In

I ought to be me
Happy as a tree
With leaves on the bole
But I feel unfree
Cooped in a black hole.

Could I walk about
I'd let out a shout
And bring down the wall
As when trumpets rang out
At Joshua's call.

Still I'm locked in
This cellar of sin
Dark as a louse.
The silence within
Would shiver a mouse.

They can't always win.
I'll risk my skin
Climb out of the night
And roused by earth's din
Set the foul place alight.

Dead Loss

Under the ground's memory
Bells are ringing
Under the sea's calvary
Children are singing.

Over the mountain's hump
The air is clearer
Over the tired heart's thump
Dear life is dearer.

After the crowning battle
There is no victory
The cut throat's rattle
Dies into history.

Lunar Aims

Where are you going to, my handsome young man?
I'm going to the moon as soon as I can
To search for a goon to drop bombs on Japan.

And where are you going to, my pretty maid?
I'm going to a swordsman to sharpen my blade
And kill a few blacks with American Aid.

And where are you going to, my Jewish boy?
I'm going to the drugstore to buy a new toy
A nice fresh gas oven for every blonde goy.

And where are you going to mavourneen, my dear?
I'm going to my boy friend to give him some gear
To wipe out a hospital and not shed a tear.

And where are you going to, my poetic friend?
I'm ploughing a waste land and going round the bend
To blow out my brains and make a fine end.

Night Noises

for Val Stavridi

I am caught in bed by wrestling winds and cries.
Flutes ripple runs, thin oboes pipe
And piccolos whistle trills on high
Like courting snipe.
Rudely a bassoon clucks and groans
Imitating a benighted hen
Or an irritable owl.
Bright clarinets are muffled by strange moans
Of saxophones.
Beside the soughing fens
Recorders write down notes with squeaking pens.
Wheezingly the voices die
And I sleep silent in my soundless soul.

Last Post

'More light!' the poet cried,
  And died.
Beauty and truth are dirty words
  Like turds
 Choked in the clogging drains
 Of hell's cloacal veins.
  Drowned are our dreams
  In lethal streams.
'More dark,' the poet sighed,
  And died.

Foundered

Stuck fast on an ironclad coast
To the jubilant cries
Of Cornish wreckers
I am lost like a ghost.
I descend among skerries
Amid drowned three-deckers
From the Spanish Main
And Indiamen from Taprobane
Weighed down by doubloons
Amassed by great tycoons
And pieces of eight
Which I cannot spend
Or lease or lend
Sundered and submerged by fate.
These are eyes that were my pearls
Glaucous unseeing eyes
Which the cruel Atlantic hurls
Into far infinities.

Shuttle Song

for Noelle and June Samuel

Every time we love
We die a little,
But love is timeless
And we are brittle.

Every time we love
We live a little,
While the potter's hands
Mix dust and spittle.

In life and in love
We grow a little,
But what we create
Time's hand will whittle.

Deep Level

I fumble in the sea-dark mine
Until iron pyrites shine
In the light of a hempen candle
On a pick-axe's handle
And dazzle my bleared eyes.
The icy waters rise
To my numbed armpits.
All around the blast
Of drilling echoes through the pits
Leaving me alone and last
As the charge detonates
In the fetid heat
And corrugating rust
With a tired heart-beat
Among loves and hates
And suffocating dust.
Why am I here brothers
Standing on these ladder rungs
Coughing up my tattered lungs
To dig treasure for the use of others
Avaricious and unjust?

God's Bones

for Roy Morrell

What are we holding that is worth while
    A red face or a barren smile?
We have lost what our fathers built
    So we make do with our own guilt.

We do not make. We wreck and we pollute
    Those things that chisel, brush and lute
Gave us to live with in those days
    When eye and ear were peeled for praise.

Knock on the door, ring at the bell,
    We'll come and answer our own hell,
But our brute heads can only grin
    And show the beast beneath the skin.

Our skin may break, but where's the butterfly?
    Caught in the coldness of our sky
We dull down to a carapace
    And bruise our dying serpent face.

Journeyman's End

for Anthony Burgess

Wandering man, stay put!
You're running in a rut
Round and around your goal
To shipwreck on a shoal.

Wandering man, stay still!
You're struggling up a hill
And roll back with your stone
Into the dread alone.

Wandering man, good night!
You've lost the beam of light
Crouching there on all fours
Behind the blackened doors.

Wandering man, have hope!
You're on an upward slope
Leading to a great field
Where the world's tombs are sealed.

At last the seals will break
And you will stand with Blake
In the bright day's delight
Far from your dungeoned night.

Star Song

A voice flowed in the desert
Below the stars whose light
Started to travel in the dirt
Of cosmic space before our sight
Began to see and hurt.
The voice took early flight
Singing in a rain of stars
The story of the human brain
And all our avatars.

Resurrection

Steady falls the rain and with each drop
I hear the guillotine go chop, chop, chop,
      And as it falls
      Each head is placed against the walls
      To make a pyramid like cannon-balls.

In days of drought the severed heads will shrink
From flesh to bone and we must think, think, think,
      Of the dog days
      When thirsty children leave their plays
      And die from wandering in a maze.

At last I hear the music of the wells
The camels coming with their bells, bells, bells,
      And all is green.
      The corpses rise so white and clean
      And break the dreaded guillotine.

Nightbreak

Down in the vale
Lilies are stale
Roses are dead
Children unfed.

By day we dwell
In a lonely hell
By night we crave
Caverns of the grave.

Up in the hills
The mountain rills
Are running dry
While children cry.

By day we tread mills
Dark wheels within wheels
By night we see stars
Between gaps in wars.

Break the cold chain
Look up again
There in the night
Heaven's alight.

Orion and Bear
Illumine the air
Ram and Goat leap
The children sleep.

Landfall

The deeper the colder it is
Until we can only see this
The submerged part
Of our iceberg heart
As the frost creaks.
The heart speaks
When there is no ache
Or icy pain
In the brain,
When warmer waves break
Against welcoming summer shores
Where the heart moors.

Recovering

We must die
That we may love one another
And learn the light.
Through darkness we grow stronger
In the healing night.
Let us live a little longer
To achieve full sight.

Night Watch

In the watches of the night.
I am thinking bright
How the jewels sound
Ticking all around
How our eyes are blind
And our shivering mind
Against the sun-blackened light
And the inward bite
That hinders our precious flight.

Transfiguration

for Edward Meryon Wilson

His face was dust
In the dry tomb
Crumbled as faces must
At their doom
Unable to see
The sky that is not there
Dead in dumb despair.
Dust gathering dust.

I lifted his bird body
Into the air
Where in the light
It took flight
And flew with flapping wings
Toward the springs
That once fed the well;
Perched in a tree
It sang a song
About right and wrong
Clear as a bell
For all to hear and see.

Out of the wood
It sang to itself a song
Of evil and good.
Then the bird flew toward the sun
Its duty done.

Fugato

for John Henniker-Major

My mind has gone off on a proleptic dance
Searching for every rhythm and nuance
That will change the arduous traffic of my soul
  Into a symphonic whole
Of sound, movement, sense and trance
   Purged from all follies of romance
Able to blow a red glow into greying coal
To invigorate, arouse and free
   While the barriers fall
   At a triumphant trumpet call,
That quality of maker within me
Which otherwise might die of ennui
   Or wither into apathy.
Words must be pungent, hot and piping
Piquant, precise, attuned and deftly leaping
   Like virgin lambs in spring
With the buried wisdom of an ancient king
   Apt to their task of shedding light
Where ignorance has been spreading night.
How else can I ever hope to sing
The song that has a heavenly ring
   Encompassing what harmony
The world can still catch from the moving sky
And the pure calm music of eternity?